# To Gaze Upon Their Loveliness

*poems by*

## Cara Chamberlain

*Finishing Line Press*
Georgetown, Kentucky

# To Gaze Upon
# Their Loveliness

*For Bernie,*
*with whom I have gazed upon many lovely creatures,*
*who have, in turn, gazed back upon us*

ACKNOWLEDGMENTS

Special thanks to Danell Jones, Tami Haaland, and Virginia Tranel for their
help with these poems. Anna Paige read "Tick Love Song" and "Elk Love
Song" on *Poetry Jam Goes Virtual* in 2020.


Publisher: Leah Huete de Maines
Editor: Christen Kincaid
Cover Art: Marian Lyman, *Blister Beetles in Hollyhocks*
Author Photo: Bernard Quetchenbach
Cover Design: Elizabeth Maines McCleavy


Order online: www.finishinglinepress.com
also available on amazon.com

Author inquiries and mail orders:
Finishing Line Press
PO Box 1626
Georgetown, Kentucky 40324
USA

# Table of Contents

*I thought of the long ages of the past, during which the successive generations of this little creature had run their course—year by year of being born, and living and dying amid these dark and gloomy woods, with no intelligent eye to gaze upon their loveliness—to all appearance such a wanton waste of beauty.*

—Alfred Russel Wallace, *The Malay Archipelago*

# Introduction

Love, it turns out, is one of the shapers of life on earth. What if Darwin's idea that female sexual selection is a driving force behind evolution—in tandem with "survival of the fittest"—had caught greater fire in our human fantasies and cultures? Would we then have foregrounded animal consciousness, choice, and beauty (the quest for which involves its own sort of violence) over power?

So let's turn Wallace's sentiment entirely around. The local people he believed were unobservant "savages" lacking an "intelligent eye" were, of course, not really savages. No human is—or we all are. And the creatures he thought were a "wanton waste" of beauty have been gazing upon their own loveliness—loveliness encompassing, for example, ultraviolet flourishes that humans cannot see—for millennia.

## Chickadee Love Song, Parts 1 and 2

1
When I grew more brain cells, I brought even stars
to orgasm, tunes pricking underwing night
like thorns. "Hey, baby,"
to every girl. Oversexed and overcharged
I was. A twit. Hawk-heckled, too. I went
darting from twig to branch.
There were a hundred guys like me: complete
maniacs—hormonally wild.
Those women so self-absorbed! Dresses
cloud-white, currant-black. The hard, snide lobe
of their critic minds measured my gifts.
And? … They weren't impressed.
God pitied Job's boils,
but the women hardly looked at me.

2
She hardly—but …
One final snap from her: she's in
my pumping wings, the wreath
of my fanned tail. Hearts fast as hailstones.
Cloaca everting in amazing vent.
Genius song—a hip-hop score,
greatest of all time—skin to lores,
lick of primaries, coverts, the cupola
of plumage I grew for this—
a second or two
on the bough
before the cat schemes a kiss
of destruction. Just a few
will fledge. But aren't we something?

✹

*In the springtime, a young male bird's brain grows new neurons to help him sing. The theory is that survival over fall and winter requires less energy be spent to support complex (and, at that time, unnecessary) brain activity, so the neurons die back. It is as if Caruso, in the off-season, forgot how to sing, but, come carnival time, he was back at the opera in perfect voice, perhaps amazing even himself. (Ornithologists are paying more attention now to the emerging realization that female birds also sing.)*

## Elk Love Song

Flutist of the avant-garde. Biggest. Worst.
Threw away his freedom.
Doesn't eat or think. Quick to take
offense, he drives us higher, faster, lunging
if we stop too long, nap, or scratch. He raises
his head to smell our pee, and, paranoid,
he doubts our loyalty. Mr. Sensitive.
Crisping days make him even worse.

We just want to get by.
Use him to keep the young guys off.
He mounts earnestly,
drops the fluty bedroom song.
When we give him to winter, he's ghostly.
By spring, calves will graze through his bones.

☀

*In the western United States in the fall, bull elk or wapiti gather
large harems of cows, whom they regularly inspect for readiness
to mate. The bulls, sporting gigantic racks, will chase off rival
males and emit unearthly "bugling" calls. In fact, they are so
busy keeping their harems together that they rarely eat, and, by
winter, when the mating season is over, they are often in poor
physical condition, easy prey for predators or simply for the
harsh conditions of deep snow and meager forage.*

## Tick Love Song

A bit engorged, she wobbled on eight small legs
into the field of my right-flank eye—larger
than that. She filled everything: gray
swell of scutum, first blood meals charging
our synganglia at once with a flash of lust,
our palps and abdominal festoons aquiver.
I can't tell you how we managed, but I grasped
the strange fate that led through eddies, a river
furred and curled, the cowlicks, the clearings, to the tucked
white tip where we clung together
on the edge of doom oscillating.
I was tweezed, but she, unmoved, I think, sucked
five hundred times her weight in blood, conquered
mischance and dropped, our thousand eggs in play.

᠅

*Dog tick: carrier of Rocky Mountain spotted fever. Deer tick: Lyme disease vector. Still, mightn't one tick look beautiful to another? They are actually quite ingeniously built. Ticks have eyes on their flanks, between the first and second legs on each side of their bodies. Their scutum is that patterned shell on the top of the thorax that you can see, often with a sinking feeling, when you find one feeding on your arm or ankle. Their palps are the two bulbous appendages that protect their mouths and look like heads, which they really don't have. That's where the synganglia come in. These are bunches of nerves near the esophagus (who knew ticks even had esophagi?). As a side note, we once tweezed 64 ticks from our dog Luke over the course of one week.*

## Mallard Duck Love Song

I've kept my eye on that one—
his water jet. Then
a head shake hot duckweed green,
a pulsed come-on. Did I mention
his chestnut, the wash on his breast,
and two sexy black curls
on his tail? And that thing he does
with his beak? Arching his neck, athletic?

It's enough to make a woman expand
secret blue spaces of her wing. But *listen,*
*he's not in love. You know the type.*
*He'll grab your neck, rip your feathers, push you*
*under. Penis a long, coiled assault—what you thought*
*was love is only kinetic.*

※

*Mallard love can be violent. Often, at the end of the mating season,*
*you'll see ducks with bare necks where the drakes have held them and*
*even pushed them down in or under the water to cruelly mate with*
*them. Fortunately, according to Richard O. Prum in his fascinating*
*book* The Evolution of Beauty: How Darwin's Forgotten Theory of
Mate Choice Shapes the Animal World—and Us, *the females are*
*not without some recourse. While drakes have developed large, curled*
*penis-like appendages, the females have countered with convoluted,*
*defensive internal anatomy. They also often choose to mate with*
*peaceable drakes, with whom they form at least temporary pair*
*bonds. The boorish behavior of unattached males is thus discouraged*
*both anatomically and socially. Prum theorizes that the female birds*
*are slowly selecting for more seemly conduct.*

## Earthworm Love Song

sediment   lime   phosphorus   sphagnum
planet's breast    scenic soil kingdom
alone   segmented   innocent
shedding frass    until it happens—clitellum boil
my mother/father said
that belt I'd never understood would turn
fiery   and ache   and you were near
with lovely genders   sidled close   yearning for
the wedding arch    we crawled through    tail-/
headfirst    egg pore    sperm pore    each giving
the halves of us male/
female    living double

❂

*If you look at an earthworm, you'll see a broad, smooth stretch of skin near one end or the other—the head, actually. This part of the earthworm—the clitellum—produces a sticky material for gathering and holding eggs during mating. Moreover, earthworms are hermaphroditic.*

## Yangtze Giant Softshell Turtle Love Song

Four. Three males and me. At the end of time.
It's so mundane: eat, drink, swim. Bask
in the prison yard. And it's not so bad, the captive
state. Ground meats suit me. I never ask
for more. Prison is politics—
so the keeper goes on about the tasks
of small souls. My companion ages,
incapable. We nod, and we go on as well.

What sorry circles, really, we describe
in the mucky stultifying pond they made
for us. It's been years. Back and forth,
sunning, celibate—not by design.
We're staring at extinction. You'd say
I don't know the unfertilized ache.

❋

*Captive in a Chinese zoo, the only known female Yangtze giant softshell turtle—at 81, perhaps the last mother of her species— and her older male companion have not produced viable eggs. Two males remain in Vietnamese zoos, but political differences between the two countries keep these duos separated. Artificial insemination, therefore, may be the species' only means of survival.*

## Slug Love Song

Was my place (my her/my his)—this plot
of land and slime, and luck, of dewy leaf
the moon shone through. We don't grieve,
my kind. By passion's knurled pollen,
there could be salt or copper and desiccation.
Or two gelid sexes blooming
extruding genitalia. Bluish moon
of sperm and ova. Then apophallation!

Tango-tangled, we stretched to part but—
so mobius, couldn't
know which was self or find an end.
Maze, the way things are, in dripping sedge.
Steeled for it, last elevation: hes
cutting off what's he, making two pearled shes.

❀

*Slugs are hermaphrodites and can become so tangled in each
other's phalluses that they have to amputate them. This is called
"apophallation."*

## Human Love Song to Earth
*(on the occasion of the anniversary of the agricultural revolution)*

My hand spans your wealth of galaxies.
My head bursts with synaptic energies.
The pinnacle of life, tops, apex, best,
language-maker, crafter now of the test
all species take—lose or pass—arbiter
of afterlives, fence-builder, atom-splitter,
dam-raiser, hunter, ploughman, president.
I am that I am—sinister, intelligent.
I never rest. I like the killing.
I like the raping. I like death and drilling
your soft guts out. My religions do
apocalypse sacraments. I've sucked you
dry in just 10,000 years. Next?
Shave you, flay you of all context.

**Queen Ant Love Song**
   *(on Wordsworth's birthday)*

Untested phantom of delight, alone
I was dormant, a capsule. All I knew
were clay and roots until adolescence grew
unbearable, and I debuted. The drones
and I—new, upper-class, winged—flirted
to heaven. They chased me, most
fell back. One or two caught up, the lost,
that is. Post-nuptial swarm? They kaputted.
I pocketed their sperm and tore my wings,
my wedding lace, and—captive queen—that was that.
You know, I could live for thirty years,
prisoner of that long-done set of flings,
except, in secret moods, I push some out:
spermless copies of me, unfathered girls.

☼

*Some "queen" ants do not need to use sperm to give birth to female
young. And, incidentally, it's strange to think of an animal that can
only sit and reproduce as some sort of sovereign, isn't it?*

## Zebra Longwing Butterfly Love Song

I don't come out,
barely metamorphosed, lie
younger than new, in doubt
of sky and wings when the guy
is rough, stabs through my silk,
cradle no sanctuary, wound
as the day it came full milk-
white from inside when I lay me down.

> *(With a will to love her,*
> *I pulled her baby bed*
> *aside, dear wings curled in birth,*
> *and gave my sacred sperm.)*

After I broke free, I bled
as imagos will, brown drops of earth.

☼

*A male zebra longwing butterfly will mate with the female adult*
*even before she emerges from her chrysalis.*

## Jellyfish Love Song

Born of sex, once under Mother's arm,
I float, cilia-powered, the sea
carrying me, my small flat form
helpless. Nothing else then but land, be
twisted, reshaped, turn polyp, and stick.
Ambition? Filter, eat, surrounded
by alter egos I bud off—more, more.
But now this happens: my rounded
topmost stalk becomes a girl medusa
born to pump waves, to take
sweets my parents knew. She'll come and come,
ribbons flowing loose.
The babies she'll make will polyp like me.
All for all, we have no "zero sum."

※

*In the class Cnidaria, jellyfish reproduce by alternating generations.
The "first" generation reproduces sexually, creating a larva that
becomes an anchored polyp, which, in turn, asexually creates an
ephyra, a free-swimming male or female medusa. Medusae mate to
begin the process all over again.*

## Red-Tailed Hawk Love Song

envy
our ceiling—sky-
light to ionosphere ::
quasars humming :: balcony ::
wild purple virga in
wavering linens ::
bed dropping, rising, spilling
to chutes over billowed
junipers—and the slide
wings make, fighting
swallow channels, gnats crystalline ::
primaries tangling talon
hook :: banded belly
to claw—nothing easy

❀

*Prairie, open sky, prickly pear in lemon and amber bloom,
bentonite cliff: two red-tailed hawks grapple, fall, rise, shout.
And the rain never quite reaches earth.*

## Anglerfish Love Song

Pressure, that darkness. Cold, empty depths
no place for regret. I followed my light—
the blue marquee read: Come and Be Kept.
Frozen mako, diatom rain, once bright
now dead fell through my ragged row
of teeth. Sometimes I danced for the viperfish,
sometimes for myself. I whirled under the undertow,
lured and scarfed whatever passed. Sans swish,

he came, bit down, embedded. We fused.
He disappeared in me—all but his testes.
I'm not sure I felt the next crawl in
and like the other become my flesh. My loves,
my parasitic boys, I've got you—or you seized me,
more than husbands—under my skin.

※

*Male anglerfish are tiny compared to the females. Consequently, they can attach themselves to a much larger mate, are basically absorbed into her body, and never have to look through the benthic realms for another chance meeting. A given female might host numerous such consorts.*

## Insect Love Song

flight-made vortex    knotted
whirled from Queen Anne's lace    along hackberries
or farther where clouds' low ferries
skid butterfly tides    forewing-clots
human, you wondered as a kid    "Hey what
are those dragonflies doing stuck together
a blue unicycle sort of tether?"

willing or not doesn't matter
notice the sky at all and see spider roads
of weavings    along those    mayflies copulating
their one day of life    moths riding cottonwood
even chafer beetles    —unaerodynamic zing—
and awkward bees do it    air alone could

☀

*When I was a kid, dragonflies, I was told, could "sew up" your lips. My husband learned it differently: they could "sew up" your ears. In fact, dragonflies, in my experience, are pretty harmless to people, but they are excellent predators of other insects. To mate, the male grasps the female behind the thorax, and she lifts the tip of her abdomen to be impregnated by his. They do this quite out in the open.*

## Swordfish Love Song (A Sonnet Crown)

*The photos, taken from a boat in incredibly clear water... are poignant: From 10 meters underwater fishermen hoist a female, whose body cavity is visibly dilated to release eggs, to the surface. As they do, a male, unrelenting in his courtship, accompanies her forced ascent and swims at her side.*
　　　　　　—Matías A. Loewy, "Mystery of Male Swordfish
　　　　　　Courtship Ritual Revealed," *Scientific American*

1
The He-Fish

She bursts, blushing, fading, through shallows,
pulled by mechanisms beyond reason,
light hard and no return, a gallows
where ambition dangles. To the myth of seasons
that sometimes infects our darkest richness
with algal choke, dead calm, or purulent storm,
up they haul her, pectorals taut, priceless
heated brain's desire, lover I'd kill for.
We all would: shark, marlin, novelist.
Goddess, mother, world, death—her side
so long and shining. Her blue eyes missed
my deficiencies. Now she's apotheosized
where milt won't. Me? A wuss, damned skipjack,
I pray her back—

2
The He-Fish

　　　　　　　　　—so I lose my faith.
There is no back. There'll be no eggs.
My circling holds. A wraith
of what I might have been, final dregs,

masculine, punk, useful only with her—
superfluous and cheap,
I bobble near her last blurred
struggle, its imprint deep.
Shall I tell you her passion,
diamonds fracturing as she fought?
Her inclination,
I flatter myself, was to shine for me. Caught
and hooked, she writhed, stabbing—what pique!
My flesh proved weak—


3
The He-Fish

                        —she died, strange nowhere
jolting her away.
I hate to think of "out there."
I pray, close by,
should she break free, I'd attend
to her, but, in truth, I drift
into the larger bent,
the sea's wish to which I fit.
I knew her gills, scales, glisten, and tail,
knew her as the incandescent sense,
caudal perfection, salvation of males.
She died for my sins?
How trite. As much as me,
she wanted that procreative spin—

4
The Photographer

        —the "mourning" male
I digitize. 1/3200 of a second—
flashing in vertical
duo with his love, their "tragedy" (I'll caption it) a small
beacon in an otherwise incomprehensible sea.
Sometimes I think of myself as a voyeur,
turning to design another's grief.
They're just fish, it's true, and, to be sure,
this is art. It's hard to be detached,
working the worst conditions, sometimes a wild
storm. Then matched
with this mechanism I've beguiled
myself into believing is self-aware—
in love?—what of this disaster can I bear?


5
The Remora

        —as the girl I clung to
goes through closed gates of the world?
Not one of those involved has a clue
about my disaster, not even, I'll guess, her.
Call me swordfish sucker, remora, hitchhiker
and general adventurer. She seemed
a good bet, vast and smooth. I liked her
right away and so I stuck myself on, dreamed
we'd go forever, plunging benthic pressure
in ways I'd never dare alone. I hung
to the gills, held there, then, bless her,
slid to a flank. For years, I clung.
But now, my vessel, my captain,
I'm off to find new friction—

6
The Sport Fisherman

         —for that alone I booked this trip,
no more stupid office geek.
Brochures promised a boat, some sun,
a bit of ego-building sport, a manhood tweak.
I'm seasick.
Things were okay until we hooked the fish.
Now I'm supposed to be quick.
Like they say, be careful what you wish.
I did research:
tied to chairs, some Hemingway types broke their arms
wrangling their trophies-of-a-lifetime.
Hyperbole, I thought, laughed. Harm is
this monster. Can't stop. The devil's due
I've paid for a damned photo op—


7
The She-Fish

         —someone else's voodoo,
I twisted, pulled, fought harder than a crew
of men. I lost. And my Andromeda
cloud of eggs is lost. Meta-
phor and real. Part for the whole. That's me.
A symbol: dying oceans, human greed.
All I want is this hook taken out,
to swim back with the foolish spawning
boy. How touching
that he follows. Sword aloft now, gills' ruching,
useless, the air-crush caving-in,
I never thought I'd leave the sea, begin
punching sun, a heat we only tell of,
a goddess's destiny, blistering.

*When he went deep-sea fishing, would Hemingway have thought himself so heroic if he'd been told that he was pitting his muscles against a bunch of women? Though it wasn't known in Hemingway's day, biologists have discovered that adult female swordfish are generally much larger than males. And, of course, Hemingway was after the largest fish he could find.*

## Nature Red in Tooth and Claw

Tennyson fatally misconstrued
the meadow's ambience when he called gutted
innards, broken femurs, everything crude,
an excuse for colonial guttings, glutted
beasts shrieking to birth his battle for the true.
Didn't he know bluebird loves bluebird in azure wings?
Lioness grips lion; tiger snarls the croon
of sex. Worm, lizard, cricket. Blister beetle bling.
It's love, not war. It's a world of lust.
Drought rolls, Sir Alfred, the desert's climax,
clouds quicken the iron hills, forests
treble with thrush desire, then an attack
of birth—what a fluty chorus
of orgiastic frogs, the snoggle, suck, egg sack.

✻

*Alfred, Lord Tennyson, might have found the lasciviousness
of nature's creatures even more troubling than their presumed
bloodthirstiness.*

## Jaguar Love Song

How with retractable claws of my fingers
I traced branching veins below your skin
from meaty wrist to elbow bend to shoulder
and it's pointless to ask, "Do you remember when . . .?"

But there's a time by the river—we
tell such legends of One—when I don't care
how the facets stab and bruise, free
of pride, we become what we are:

two killers in love, rosettes afire
as you bite my neck (100 times)—ecstatic
strangers' pelage, tectonic wire,
shock collision, not (NOT!) merely loved, the lick,

the claw, the bruise … and peace. And here I thought
I'd die to you, orange ice and hot.

❋

*This poem is not meant to stereotype cat mating rituals. Apparently, some jaguars are quite gentle with each other and may form a conjugal partnership for quite a while: https://www.youtube.com/ watch?v=8quTixw-R8I.*

Born and raised in Salt Lake City, Utah, **Cara Chamberlain** grew up hiking in the Wasatch and Uinta Mountains, learned to birdwatch along the bays and inlets of the Great Salt Lake, and attended the University of Utah, where she received her BA in English. At Purdue University, she earned an MA in Creative Writing. Subsequently, she and her husband and son moved to Wyoming, Maine, and Florida. She taught at Northwest College in Powell, Wyoming; at the University of Maine at Fort Kent; at Université de Moncton, campus d'Edmundston in New Brunswick, Canada; and at Florida Southern College in Lakeland. In 2006, Cara and her husband moved to Billings, Montana, where she taught at Rocky Mountain College and Montana State University Billings. She is currently a free-lance copyeditor.

The author of *Hidden Things, The Divine Botany,* and *Lament of the Antichrist in a Secular World and Other Poems,* Cara has published in numerous journals and anthologies, including *Nimrod, Boston Review, The Southern Review, Poems Across the Big Sky,* and *Poetics for the More-Than-Human World.* She has received four Pushcart Prize nominations and been a finalist in the Ashland Poetry Press, Lo-Fi Novella, and Blue Light Book Award contests.

Cara is a conservationist and advocate for animals of all kinds. She supports native-plant and pollinator-friendly gardening, has run afoul of city zoning, and has served on the board of the Yellowstone Chapter of Montana Conservation voters.